STILL CAN'T BREATHE

Still Can't Breathe: Unbelievable Deception

Printed in the United States of America
Keen Vision Publishing, LLC
www.publishwithkvp.com
ISBN: 979-8-9992130-4-4

STILL CAN'T BREATHE

UNBELIEVABLE DECEPTION

KEEN VISION PUBLISHING

Deborah Laster

CONTENTS

INTRODUCTION

We live in an era where events and scenarios are not always as they appear. Why is that? There are numerous reasons; however, the rise of technology and artificial intelligence (AI) makes us question reality, fantasy, truth, and lies. We refuse to acknowledge and accept the truth when it is revealed. Depending on the topic, we would rather believe a lie over the truth. However, whether we choose to believe the truth or a lie, it will NOT eradicate the issue at hand. Nothing in this world is what you think it is. Everything is a smoke screen. The world is a stage. We have been ultimately deceived.

Listen as Wisdom calls out! Hear as Understanding raises her voice! On the hilltop along the road, she takes her stand at the crossroads. She cries aloud by the gates at the entrance to the town, on the road leading in: *"I call to you, to all of you! I raise my voice to all people. Use good judgment, you simple people. You foolish people, show some understanding."*

Foolish people care only about themselves; they lash out at common sense. Fools are not interested in understanding; they only want to air their opinions. Listen to Wisdom! She has important things to tell you. Wisdom speaks the truth. She detests every kind of deception. Choose her instructions rather than silver and her knowledge rather than pure gold. Common sense and success belong to Wisdom. Insight and strength are hers. Whoever finds her finds life and receives favor from the LORD. But those who miss her injure themselves. For the fear of the LORD is the beginning of wisdom.

For so long, we so-called Black people have been trying to figure out who we are and what part of Africa we originated. We have used websites like Ancestry.com to discover our heritage, gain insight into our DNA, and trace our family history. Yet, we — particularly those who are Christians — never once thought to start at the beginning. You might say, "The beginning of what?"

The Bible says, *"In the beginning, God created the heavens and the earth"* (Genesis 1). The answer to all questions has always been in the Bible. One of my old pastors out of Texas would occasionally make this statement: "Everything you want to know about life is in the Bible." For many years, I pondered that very statement and have come to know that it was then and still today a true statement.

When you start with the Bible and really think about it, you will realize how it makes sense. God started with the first two people – the creation of Adam and Eve. The Bible breaks down the descendants of all nations of people. This breakdown was on purpose. These nations of families did not simply die off but continue to live through all generations of nations existing today. Therefore, every individual living today should be able to trace their lineage in the Bible. We know that the Most High God flooded the Earth, killing all human beings except for eight people – Noah, his wife, their three sons, and their wives. Noah's sons were Shem,

Ham, and Japheth, whom God used to repopulate the Earth. All people living today are descendants of one of these three sons.

But for some reason, when you try to bring simple logic to people's minds, they tend to lack common sense. Common Sense has died in the world, particularly in America and particularly in the black community. Common Sense lives by simple, sound reasoning and understanding. Common Sense began to deteriorate rapidly when overbearing regulations were put in place. The government passes laws to legalize and highly encourage same-sex marriages. Common Sense lost ground when drag queens started story-time reading to preschool and elementary school children, but Christians cannot come into the school and read Bible stories to the children. We declined even further as children are now being taught gender fluidity, and all parental rights are being taken from parents.

Common Sense lost the will to live once churches became social and financial institutions, citizens were allowed to loot and rob stores, and women were allowed to murder their unborn babies under the deception of "reproductive rights." Common Sense took a beating when illegal immigrants flooded into America and began to have more rights than actual American citizens. Common Sense was preceded in death by his parents, Truth and Holiness; his wife, Righteousness; his daughter, Freedom; and his son, Justice. Common Sense is survived by three stepsiblings: "My Body, My Choice," Transgender Rights, and Support Israel.

We live in a generation that has been brainwashing the minds of the masses. We have been psychologically programmed via social engineering, with years of subliminal messages through television, music, intimidation, manipulation, and domination. This is on purpose and by design. We must wake up and become aware of Satan's plans and strategy. We must get our heads out of the sand and pay attention to what's happening around us. We must not take everything we hear on the news as truth. We must learn again how to use our common sense. Because we lack common sense, we lack principles and moral standards. Proverbs 14:12 (KJV) says, *"There is a way which seemed right unto a man, but the end thereof are the ways of death."*

The heart of this book is to unveil the many lies that many of us have believed to be truth. I desire to instill revelation, inspiration, and illumination in the heart and mind of the reader. I am not asking you to believe what you read in this book, but instead, ponder, think about it, and consider it. I highly recommend that you research and search out the matter for yourself.

THE ART OF DECEPTION

The word deception means to err, go astray, wonder, to seduce, to be led from the path of virtue to sin, to sever or fall away from the truth; to be led away into error; to roam away from safety. An example of a figure of deception is Satan. Revelations 12:9 (KJV) says, *"And the great dragon was cast out, that old serpent, called the Devil, and Satan, which deceiveth the whole world."* Satan, through false teachers, has twisted God's word. Most Americans are oblivious to the real truth surrounding the issues of life and of the world.

Satan comes on Earth and accuses you within your conscience. His greatest tool is deception because he has no real power (Colossians 2:15). John 8:44 tells us how Satan is the father of lies. Satan does not give us time to guard our minds against him. He starts early and in ways we do not realize. We have been fed lies since the start of the public education system and have come to believe these lies. We are no longer educated; we are INDOCTRINATED. The Bible tells us that God's people are destroyed for lack of knowledge—why? Because we reject knowledge (Hosea

4:6). This knowledge we reject is the B-I-B-L-E.

First, we must address and correct one thing we have all been duped into believing: The Bible is NOT a religious book. It is not about religion. Religion can be explained as a set of beliefs concerning the cause, nature, or purpose of the universe. In other words, religion is man's attempt to reconnect to Heaven through culture and traditions. Religion was not introduced or created by the Most High. It is a deception of Satan. Why would a one and only Supreme God have many religions? The Bible is about establishing a government or a culture of Heaven on Earth. The Bible is about the Kingdom of Heaven and the Kingdom of God. The Kingdom of Heaven is a place or the invisible Kingdom, and the Kingdom of God is the culture of Heaven.

God, the creator of Heaven and Earth, decided that as the King of Heaven, He wanted to expand His territory to the Earth. He also decided that He would extend His territory and establish the same authority and culture on Earth as it is in Heaven. God, the creator of Heaven, Earth, and all humankind, had the sole purpose of giving man authority and dominion on Earth as long as they obeyed His rules and laws. This obedience is about coming to the knowledge of this truth and transforming your ideology to align with God's way of thinking, choosing to submit to His laws and not our own will or the enemy's, Satan's, deception.

We have been programmed to believe a lie. It is not a coincidence that our TV shows are also called "programs." The word "program" is defined as providing a computer or machine with coded instructions for the automatic performance of a task. Your TV is nothing more than an electronic, mind-altering device. It has been designed to psychologically change the ways you view reality. Thus, ignorance is man's first problem because the start of deception occurs first in the mind.In tackling ignorance, we must confront a harsh reality that many of us have been avoiding—we have been lied to. This world, under the sway of the devil, has deceived us into believing that this earthly life is all that matters. From the day we are born, we are bombarded with messages that emphasize the importance of world success and material gain . We are told to get a good education, be career-focused, buy a house, fall in love, and accumulate wealth. While these are not bad things, the emphasis placed on them often blinds us to the deeper truth of our existence.

The Bible warns us about the deceiver, Satan, who is described as the "god of this world" and the "prince of the power of the air." These titles are not mere words but reveal the extent of Satan's influence over this world. Satan has a significant level or method of control, and he uses it to lie to the masses. His greatest deception is convincing us that this life is all that matters—that our primary focus should be all about success and material gain. This lie has infiltrated even within our churches.

Many sermons today focus on prosperity and material things. Satan has lied to us, making us prioritize temporary pleasures over the eternal prize. The prosperity gospel has further propagated this lie, making us believe that we can have all the world's riches and all of God at the same time. God is not Santa Claus. He is not here to fulfill our every material desire. Through Satan's deception, we have been convinced to focus on the here and now, casting our eyes on every shiny thing around us. However, the wealth we have accumulated or the status we have achieved has no merit without a relationship with the Most High God. Our primary focus should be on our spiritual health and relationship with God.

The world is shaped to keep the masses busy and distracted, forcing our eyes away from God, whom we should focus on. Satan is highly skilled in the art of distraction. It is one of the most subtle and surprising weapons in his arsenal, which is designed to lure us away from our true faith. As Christians, we cannot allow ourselves to conform to the culture of this world (Romans 12:2). It will only lead us astray and cause us to follow the wrong path, getting closer and closer to the deceiver.

Those who operate and align themselves under Satan are the antichrist. The antichrist's every action will be part of a grand design to deceive and control. He will manipulate global events to create crises that only he can solve, further solidifying his position of power in a way that appears beneficial but ultimately serves his dark purposes. This calculating series of deception will be so convincing that even the most discerning individual may be tempted to believe in his false promises. We must actively fight against this deception!

Americans like to idle around the truth nowadays, which we do by labeling ourselves relativists. Like Pontius Pilate, we ask, "What is truth?" with the implication being that truth exists only in the eye of the beholder. In the political realm, this preference for opinion rather than facts means that many of us debate our positions by covering our ears, closing our eyes, and shouting at one another. So, when truth does come shambling along to whap us upside the head, we are inevitably shocked. The truth may set us free, but oftentimes, our first encounter with truth usually incites a reaction that leads to violence, confusion, and, most often, denial.

Thus, consider 1 Timothy 2:4 (KJV), which reads, *"God our Saviour, who will have all men to be saved, and to come unto the knowledge of the truth."* We must call upon God and depend on His wisdom and grace. We have to choose to align ourselves with His purpose consciously. Roman 12:2

(KJV) reminds us, *"And be not conformed to this world: but be ye transformed by the renewing of your mind."* How does someone renew their mind? By reading the word of God.

Everyone thinks they know the truth and believes what we hear on the daily news is true. **NEWSFLASH!** If what you have grown to know, as it relates to life and the way of life, and what you now know, does not align with the Bible, then you may want to reconsider some things. And for those of us who profess to be Christian, please read your Bible. The Bible holds the truth. Christianity is dominated and saturated with pagan ideology and doctrine.

Many of the things we have been taught in church for most of our lives were not based on what the Bible teaches but rather on traditions. Colossians 2:8 (KJV) states, *"Beware lest any man spoil you through philosophy and vain deceit, after the tradition of men, after the rudiments of the world, and not after Christ."* These "traditions of men" have become so commonplace that few people question them or even think about questioning them. You worship the Anti-Christ/Beast System/Government by bowing down in submission to his command and his laws.

The psychological warfare against humanity is as such:

- Manipulation: *We will pay you.*
- Intimidation: *We will fire you.*
- Domination: *We will control you.*

This group will work relentlessly to:

- Control the press.
- Corrupt the youth through sex and drugs.
- Elect their own people to have key positions in all levels of government.

The final goal is to take over the world, forming the New

World Order. Reflect on this quote from Manly Palmer Hall, where he states:

> *When the human race learns to read the language of symbolism, a great veil will fall from the eyes of men. They shall then know the truth, and more than that, they shall realize that from the beginning, truth has been in the world unrecognized, save by a small but gradually increasing number appointed by the Lords of the Dawn as ministers to the needs of human creatures struggling to regain their consciousness of divinity.*

AMERICA

(MYSTERY BABYLON THE GREAT, REV 17:5)

America is a wolf in sheep's clothing. God wants to expose the lies embedded in the fabric of our society. The United States is controlled and manipulated by a private foreign power, and our unlawful Federal United States Government is their pawnbroker. We must first look at and analyze the seat of power in America to understand how deep the deception runs.

Washington, D.C., was established as a city-state in 1871 with the passage of the Act of 1871, officially establishing the United States as a corporation under the rule of Washington, which itself is subservient to the City of London. Washington was initially named Rome, Maryland. The landowner renamed Goose Creek to Tiber Creek, transitioning from European inspiration to American reality. This act mirrored Rome's iconic River Tiber, creating a symbolic link across continents. The landowner's vision was to merge ancient Rome's grandeur with America's budding potential. Rome disseminated into the European nations and conquered America. Therefore, America is an extension of the old Roman Empire.

The City of London, Vatican City, and Washington, D.C. are sovereign, corporate entities not connected to the nations they appear to be part of. In other words, the City of London is not technically part of Greater London or England, just as Vatican City is not part of Rome or Italy. Likewise, Washington DC is not part of the United States it controls. These sovereign, corporate entities have their own laws and their own identities. They also have their own flags. There is no democracy. These are the trinity of globalist control: Vatican City — Religion, under the Pope, to control the beliefs, minds, and spirituality of humanity; City of London — Finance, King Charles, the courts, and banks to control the money/bonds; Washington, DC — Military, under the Elite government, Military to quash rebellion and act as the world police. All three have Egyptian obelisks.

In 1868, Washington, D.C., was incorporated in Delaware as a privately owned company, and today, we are all employees of a corporation called the United States. Corporations are run by presidents, which is why we call the person perceived to hold the highest seat of power in the land "the president." The fact is, the president is nothing more than a figurehead for the central bankers and transnational corporations, who ultimately control this country and call the shots.

Unfortunately, history is not as we have come to know it. European immigration to America had NOTHING to do with seeking religious liberty. We have been told that America's Founding Fathers established the country under a Christian doctrine. The notion that this country's roots are explicitly Christian is both foolish and false. The United States was not founded on the Lord Jesus Christ, as we have all been led to believe. Yes, it was founded on God, but whose and what god? The premise that the United States was founded on Christianity is a mere smokescreen.

Ask yourself, "What is Christianity?" According to Google, it is the religion based on the person and teachings of Jesus of Nazareth or its beliefs and practices. The Jesus that I know does not advocate the dehumanized treatment of any individual. The Jesus that I know does not advocate same-sex marriages. The Jesus that I know does not advocate Planned Parenthood, including abortions (aka Moloch sacrifice). The Jesus that I know does not advocate pagan holidays. Therefore, perceiving or insisting that the Founding Fathers were Christians is an oxymoron. On the contrary, they were all a part of an organization, Freemasonry; it had the teachings and practices of the secret fraternal (men only) order of Free and Accepted Masons, the largest worldwide secret society, which has nothing in common with our Lord Jesus Christ.

The Pope is the Godfather of America. Rome was the seat of power for the Roman Empire, and the Pope continues to hold this seat. Rome, Maryland, was the original name of a community within Prince George's County, Maryland, which eventually became Washington, DC. The property that would become the site of the United States Capitol Building was inscribed as "Rome" in the Maryland property records in 1663. George Washington, Thomas Jefferson, and others not only adopted systems of government and law from the classical, mainly Roman, world, but they also built a capital city that first echoed ancient Rome and then later Athens in its architecture, sculpture, and painted interiors. The White House is a replica of an ancient Roman temple.

Therefore, the United States government is actually a Roman government. Everything we are was built around Roman culture and government. We have a U.S. Senate on Capitol Hill, just as the Romans had a senate. Washington, D.C., was known as Rome before the name changed to

Washington, D.C., because America is an extension of the "new" Roman Empire along with the European nations.

America is more than just evil. It was and still is a declaration of war against God and his chosen people (detailed in my book, "I Can't Breathe, Don't Die Twice"). Do not fall for the propaganda shoved down your throats! The reality of America is not in "God we trust" but rather in "Paganism (Lucifer) we trust." The deep dive into the back of the dollar bill may further shock you because money has a rather telling paper trail.

On December 23, 1913, the Federal Reserve (neither federal nor a reserve as it is a privately owned institution) was created. A group of bankers and politicians planned it at a secret meeting in 1910 on Jekyll Island, Georgia. This move transferred the power to create money from the American Government to a private group of bankers.

Throughout history, we have been taught that this government has been established to protect our freedom. We have been taught that our churches are here to help support and promote a healthy, godly life in society. And we have placed our faith in these two institutions that have miserably failed us. But they both were already preset to be totally against us, to be weaponized against us. The higher-ups fed us the lie of the separation of church and state, yet our government continues to operate with the unity of church and state. Their whole premise is religion, politics, and money.

Politicians are put in place to give us the idea that we have freedom of choice. The Elites own everything. They own all the important land, they own and control corporations, and they have bought and paid for the Senate, Congress, the state houses, city hall, judges, and all media. They spend billions of dollars every year lobbying to get what they want. They don't want a population of citizens capable of critical thinking. They want obedient workers. We have let them tell us what to think and have not scratched past the surface, so they continue to feed us lies and lead us down the path of unrighteousness. They continue to utilize their sources to take away power from the citizens.

The United States is said to be in a severe deficit. However, you have to remember they create crises that send us into a tailspin. The rise of global debt is not just a series of unfortunate economic events but is part of a calculated and orchestrated plan to bring the world to its knees. This act is not a coincidence. It is a strategy designed to weaken national sovereignty and centralize power in the hands of a few. Any American who thinks they are living in a free country does not have a clue, and they need to wake up.

A DESTROYED PEOPLE

We have all heard the saying, "Knowledge is power!" Usually, when we hear the truth about something for the first time, we reject the truth because we are not familiar with the subject. It's so sad to think of how many people, especially our people, are lost because they cannot receive and accept the truth when it is presented to them.

The Bible does inform us that many will not accept the truth. Hosea 4:6 (KJV) says, *"My people are destroyed for lack of knowledge; because thou hast rejected knowledge, I will also reject thee… seeing thou hast forgotten the law of thy God, I will also forget thy children."* This scripture does not refer to all people. It is only referring to those people who were brought over into this country by way of slave ships and those Indigenous people, whom Americans want to call "Indians," who were already here.

We have been denied knowledge and information more than any other group. If you think that scripture is not referring to us, think again. This is why we have been constantly abused, exploited, killed, and utterly destroyed by the other nations. Deuteronomy 28:15-28 outlines the atrocities of those who experienced slavery in America. We are the children of the Most High God, which has nothing to do with your salvation (although all people need a savior) but has everything to do with our bloodline, being that we are the ancestors of Abraham, Isaac, and Jacob.

Of course, those reading this might be thinking to yourself, "If we are the true children of the Most High God, then who are those people in Israel?" I am glad you asked that question. Your Bible states in Revelation 2:9 (NKJV), *"And I know the blasphemy of those who say they are Jews and are not, but are a synagogue of Satan."* The Bible does not mention it once but several times. In the next chapter, it brings up the people in Israel again. Revelation 3:9 (NKJV) says, *"Indeed I will make those of the synagogue of Satan, who say they are Jews and are not, but lie — indeed I will make them come and worship before your feet, and to know that I have loved you."*

Real history is not taught in the schools or the Babylonian CHRISTIAN churches regarding the true Hebrew people and who they are. The masses were NEVER taught that the west coast of Africa was once known as Negroland. The Negros were, in fact, brought from Africa, but what's NEVER taught is that the Negros weren't Africans; they migrated there from Israel.

The dispersion of Black Americans, aka "Judah," started in the time of 485 BC and continued through 70 AD. These men and women fled over the Atlas Mountain and passed into Morocco. Many went further into places beyond the deserts and rivers, places referred to as the wilderness back then. The nation of Israel took various routes into Africa, many into a region near the West Coast. Over a period of 1200 years, this area would become known as Negroland.

In 70 AD, Rome brought a temporary end to the nation of Israel. Burning the city of Jerusalem, bringing a great war and slaughter. Romans' hatred for Christ and vengeance on Christ's people was so great that the Hebrews migrated until they ended up on the West Coast of Africa. Christ predicted that the people would be overthrown, the Temple would be destroyed, and the Black Negros, Hebrews, would be scattered (Mat. 24:15-21, Luke 21:5-6, 20-24). The loss of life was appalling, and so many of the Hebrew people were slain that the whole lake of Galilee was red with blood and covered with corpses. The noted historian Josephus, who described the massive genocide, estimated that one million one hundred thousand perished in the siege of Jerusalem.

Once the evil European slave traders had Judah in their sights, the only place on the planet they could take them was the Americas. After causing the death of millions of Hebrews (Black Americans) during their transport to America, Europeans began the systematic destruction of Israel as a nation:

- Hebrew names were changed to European names.
- Hebrews were forced to speak English and forbidden to speak Hebrew.
- Hebrews were forbidden to read the Bible and could only learn what Europeans taught them.
- Hebrew families were split up and sold to different slave owners.
- Hebrew women were raped, and so were the men in an evil homosexual practice called "buck breaking."
- Hebrew babies were used as bait to catch alligators and sometimes for sport.

The LORD shall bring a nation against thee from far, from the end of the earth, as swift as the eagle flieth; a nation whose tongue thou shalt not understand; A nation of fierce countenance, which shall not regard the person of the old, nor shew favour to the young: And he shall eat the fruit of thy cattle, and the fruit of thy land, until thou be destroyed: which also shall not leave thee either corn, wine, or oil, or the increase of thy kine, or flocks of thy sheep, until he have destroyed thee.

DEUTERONOMY 28:49-51(KJV)

Make no mistake. This "new world" was hell on Earth for Hebrews and Native Americans. Nobody forced Europeans to commit such evil. These were conscious choices they made to side with Satan and declare war on God and His people. However, it was only the beginning of the first groups of slaves brought to America.

For almost 400 years, Europeans would continue to kidnap, rape, torture, beat, murder, and scatter Judah. The United States is a crime scene with the evidence of the people they stole. The United States was built on stolen land and sustained by stolen labor. Black Americans built the foundation of a nation claiming freedom for all. Blacks were dehumanized to justify slavery, while European Americans could pretend that they were good and righteous, so-called Christian people.

Slavery in America wasn't only about free labor, racism, and hate. Europeans specifically identified and targeted the Tribe of Judah (Black Americans) for slavery so that we could build "treasure cities," as our forefathers designed for the Egyptians in the Old Testament (Exodus 1:11). Our people have built the United States into one of the greatest nations on the planet. History shows slavery helped build many U.S. colleges and universities. Of course, it didn't stop there.

On December 14, 1711, a law passed by the New York

City Common Council made Wall Street the city's first official slave market for the sale and rental of enslaved Blacks and Native Americans. We were sold and used to create this country. We have contributed to many inventions that have revolutionized and created billions, if not trillions, of dollars in industries. To mention a few:

- **Frederick McKinley Jones** was known for his innovative mobile refrigeration technology.
- **Daniel Hale Williams** performed the 1st successful open-heart surgery.
- **Garrett Morgan's** most notable inventions were a type of three-way traffic light and a protective smoke hood.
- **Lewis Howard Latimer's** inventions included an evaporative air conditioner, an improved process for manufacturing carbon filaments for electric light bulbs, and an improved toilet system for railroad cars.
- **Percy Lavon Julian** was the first person to synthesize the natural product physostigmine and a pioneer in industrial large-scale chemical synthesis of the human hormones progesterone and testosterone from plant sterols such as stigmasterol and sitosterol.

It is a known fact that Black Americans have built this country and have built wealth for European Americans as well as for other nations. This nation has yet to fully acknowledge and tell the truth about our history—the legacy of slavery, racial terror, lynchings (the true holocaust), and literally the abuse and atrocities of Black Americans, including the genocide of Native Americans. The travesties done are numerous and scattered throughout history:

1923 – After a white woman falsely accused a black man of rape, a white mob attacked the thriving black town of

Rosewood, Florida, in a multi-day massacre that destroyed the town and left hundreds dead.

1811 – The largest slave insurrection in U.S. history began in Louisiana Territory; after their defeat, many of the 500 rebelling enslaved people were mutilated, decapitated, and burned alive.

1904 – A black man named Luther Holbert and an unidentified black woman were tortured, mutilated, and burned alive in front of 600 picnicking white spectators in Doddsville, Mississippi.

1899 – In Newman, Georgia, thousands gathered to watch the brutal lynching of Sam Hose, a black man who was mutilated and burned alive; spectators afterward gathered body parts to sell as souvenirs.

1796 – President George Washington offered a $10 reward for the return of Oney Judge, an enslaved black woman who fled after learning that Mrs. Washington planned to give her away as a wedding gift.

1944 – South Carolina electrocuted George Stinney Jr., a 90-pound, black 14-year-old, after he was falsely accused of rape and murder.

1917 – Thirteen black soldiers were executed after Houston, Texas; police beat and shot black troops, prompting 156 soldiers to revolt; in all, 19 black soldiers were hanged, and 50 of them were sentenced to life in prison.

1956 – Rosa Jordan, a pregnant black woman, was shot in both legs while riding a desegregated bus after the Montgomery Bus Boycott.

1918 – Mary Turner, an eight-month pregnant black woman who spoke out publicly against the lynching of her husband, was hanged from a tree with her head facing down, had gasoline thrown on her, and burned the clothes off her body.

She was still alive when the mob took a large butcher knife to her abdomen, cutting the unborn baby from her body and crushing the crying baby's head with one of the man's feet; afterward, they riddled her body with hundreds of bullets, killing her.

Supposedly, things changed for Black Americans after a time. However, the supposed change was only a guise. The lie that the 13th Amendment freed Black Americans has blinded most people to the fact that the American prison system is nothing more than slavery re-branded as "mass incarceration."

As Billy Graham once observed in his message "Over 200-Year Curse on Black People: The Truth They Tried to Bury," the so-called "black curse" was never divine — it was constructed. It was a lie designed by colonizers and profiteers to sever a people from their history, land, and identity. The real chains were placed on the mind and the spirit, redefining what it meant to be Black. These lies, passed down for centuries, painted strength as weakness and brilliance as shame. But every time truth is spoken, the illusion weakens. Every scar our ancestors carried was an investment in our freedom. Their silence was forced; our voices are free. The curse was never real — the brilliance in our DNA, the strength in our lineage, and the fire in our spirit are what's real. The world must now face what happens when the people they tried to bury rise with clarity, pride, and purpose.

What has happened to Black Americans was more than just evil—it was a declaration of war against the Most High God and His Chosen People.

At the time of those events," says the Lord,
"when I restore the prosperity of Judah and Jerusalem,
I will gather the armies of the world
into the valley of Jehoshaphat.
There I will judge them
for harming my people, my special possession,
for scattering my people among the nations,
and for dividing up my land.
They threw dice to decide which of my people would be their slaves.
They traded boys to obtain prostitutes
and sold girls for enough wine to get drunk.

JOEL 3:1-3 (NLT)

The nations have taken crafty counsel and devised cunning plans to destroy us (Psalm 83). It has been a distorted effort to destroy the people of the God Most High. They are trying to manipulate and alter the God DNA of our people. Tank Thinkers are at the round table, and Lab Dogs (Mad Scientists) are in their laboratory cooking and brewing up insidious satanic concoctions to defeat Christ at His return and the Children of God Most High. Their strategy is using sorcery, television (tell-a-vision), movies, music, and manipulation. They infiltrate our music to control our minds and change our way of thinking so that we will destroy our own selves. Our Bible tells us to *"Stay alert! Watch out for your great enemy, the devil. He prowls around like a roaring lion, seeking for someone to devour."*

They serve us so-called "entertainment." The etymology of the word entertainment-- Enter, from the Latin means "inside." Tain is "to grasp, to hold, to possess, occupy or control." Ment comes from men, or "the mind." The word suggests the mental state of entering and/or holding.

In other words, entertainment is allowing demonic

beings to enter inside of you to take hold of or possess your mind. There is nothing wrong with enjoying yourself and being entertained, but be careful of what that entertainment consists of.

Their whole objective is to destroy the minds of you and especially your children. They have been unsuccessful in coming against us via systemic racism and other means. Therefore, they have to come against us inwardly, causing them to be brilliantly successful in helping us destroy ourselves. They have been reprogramming us from the day we came out of our mother's womb. We have been programmed to operate in the lust of the flesh, the lust of the eyes, and the pride of life. The Bible tells us not to conform ourselves to this world, but we should transform our minds by renewing them with the word of God. We have been given a history, education, and a culture that is not our history or culture. They have been infiltrating us to disconnect us from our God-gene. They have been purposefully keeping us in sin to separate us from our God.

In the book of Numbers, Chapter 22 speaks on how after the Israelites defeated the Amorites, the king of Moab, Balak, was terrified that the Israelites would destroy his nation as well. Balak asked a prophet named Balaam to curse the Israelites. However, the Lord directed Balaam that he was not to curse the Israelites because they had been blessed! Later, Balaam disobeyed the Lord and told Balak that he could weaken the Israelites by enticing them to commit sin. Do I need to repeat what I just mentioned?

In other words, Balaam told Balak that if you manipulate their minds, deceive them into fornicating, psychologically program them, and present to them "entertainment," it will drive them to sin on their own accord; it will cause them to self-destruct whereby they will curse themselves. Like

Balaam, the higher-ups are pulling the same moves. They don't want you to know who you are and understand the power behind who you are. They want you to submerge yourself in sin and debauchery behavior. Do not buy into their predictive programming.

Predictive programming is the theory that the government or other higher-ups are using fictional movies or books as a mass mind control tool to make the population more accepting of planned future events. Predictive programming is a subtle form of psychological conditioning provided by the media to acquaint the public with planned societal changes to be implemented by our leaders. Guard yourself against these tactics. Ephesians 6:11 (AMP) instructs: "Put on the full armor of God [for His precepts are like the splendid armor of a heavily-armed soldier], so that you may be able to successfully stand up against all the schemes and the strategies and the deceits of the devil."

In their strategies and schemes against God's people, the higher-ups said to themselves, "Let's make sure some of them are rich, then we got to trick some of them to think they can get rich, such as college graduates thinking they will get rich but ending up with so much debt or ending up with a job outside their degree or no job at all." They continue to say that with the remaining few, they will dangle a carrot in front of those people and keep them chasing the carrot, never catching it. That is the so-called "American Dream"— and it was exactly that, a dream. It's all an illusion. We live in a matrix.

Consider this powerful quote from Morpheus in the movie "The Matrix," where he said, "The Matrix is a system. That system is our enemy... The Matrix is everywhere. It is all around us... It is the world that has been pulled over your eyes to blind you from the truth. That you are a slave.

Like everyone else, you were born into bondage. Born into a prison that you cannot smell or taste or touch. A prison for your mind." As I told you, everything begins in the mind.

Another example from pop culture would be the movie with Eddie Murphy called "Trading Places." For those who do not know, the movie is about a wealthy commodities broker, Louis Winthorpe III, and a street hustler, Billy Ray Valentine, who unknowingly become part of a social experiment by two wealthy brothers. The brothers switch the lives of Louis and Billy Ray to see how environment affects success, destroying Louis's life while giving Billy Ray a shot at high society.

This is what happened to us. We were switched. Why? Because our people, all through the Bible and even now, turned away from God and began to practice pagan rituals and worship pagan gods. God allowed our enemy to rule over us. This is why He said what He said to us in Hosea 6:4.

Now, consider this excerpt from author Dennine Barnett's book, "Jerusalem: Urusalima":

> *Hitler said that day the World War 3 will start, mankind will learn that I was trying to save my nation from the Free Masons, the Illuminati, and the Jews.*
>
> *Hitler asked this question to a soldier, "Do you know who America has in its possessions?*
>
> *"NO," the soldier replied.*
>
> *Hitler said, "The Americans have the jewels of God. The Americans have stolen God's precious jewels.*
>
> *"What do you mean his precious jewels?" The soldier asked.*
>
> *Hitler said, "America has stolen the Jews. The Jews of God, His Jewelry: The Negroes.*

They are the true Hebrews. What a foolish move and a direct challenge to God. And they plan on moving these false white Jews into a state of Israel. When America and its Jewish Slave masters conquer the world and the world realizes I was right, then all the nations will begin a third world war to dethrone America of its rule."

"Why will the Jews control America?" The soldier asked.

Hitler said, "Because the white Jews know that the Negroes are the real Children of Israel and to keep Americas secret the Jews will blackmail America. They will extort America. Their plans for world domination won't work if the Negroes know who they were. The White citizens of America will be terrified to know that all this time they have been mistreating, discriminating, and lynching the Children of Israel. They will fear that God will destroy them as he had destroyed Egypt for doing the exact same thing. Therefore, the Elite, the Illuminati, keep this a secret at all costs."

These examples aren't just stories from the screen or speculative excerpts from controversial texts. They are warnings. Parables. Reminders. The message is always the same if you look closely: you were never meant to know the truth. We've been conditioned. Not by accident. Not by coincidence. But by design. Our bondage isn't just physical—it's mental, generational, and intentional. The enemy didn't simply conquer our bodies. They hijacked our identity, erased our history, and reprogrammed our minds.

Malcolm X once declared:

Brothers and sisters… it's time we stop pretending that the truth can be spoken softly. When a people have been stripped of their name, language, culture, and pride, don't expect them to whisper their story. You brought them in chains, sold their children, and built a nation on their backs — then asked why they can't 'catch up.' Identity is not a gift from the oppressor; it is reclaimed by the oppressed. Speaking truth boldly is not aggression — it is self-respect. Our history did not begin with slavery. We were kings and queens before we were captives, scholars before we were shackled. Erase a people's past, and you can control their future — but our history was never lost, only hidden.

So, now the question is no longer centered on what happened to us, but what happens next.

SATAN SEED

And I will cause hostility between you and the woman, and between your offspring and her offspring. He will strike your head, and you will strike his heel.

GENESIS 3:15 (NLT)

In this verse, God speaks to Satan after the deception in Eden, issuing the first prophecy of Christ's victory over evil. The "woman" symbolizes faithful Israel (Isaiah 54:5–6), and her seed is Christ, whom Satan sought to destroy (Matthew 2:2). Though the Serpent would wound Him, Christ would ultimately crush Satan's head (Romans 16:20). Those who live according to Satan's desires are his children (John 8:44); those who continue in sin belong to him (1 John 3:8). Satan's influence extends through powerful individuals and institutions that advance his agenda.

Figures such as the Rothschilds, Rockefellers, Bilderbergers, George Soros, Henry Kissinger, Bill Gates, and even the Vatican have operated through systems like Freemasonry and secret societies to oppose Christ's kingdom. Their job is to create chaos in the world, thereby ushering in the New World Order (NWO). No one will enter the

New World Order unless they pledge to worship Satan. For centuries, Satan has used his followers to devise a plan to deceive the whole world and take over planet Earth. Divide and conquer is the strategy of the elites. If they can keep the population divided, they can divide, conquer, and control. These people hold all the wealth.

> *I know thy works, and tribulation, and poverty, (but thou art rich) and I know the blasphemy of them which say they are Jews and are not, but are the synagogue of Satan.*
> **REVELATION 2:9 (KJV)**

> *Behold, I will make them of the synagogue of Satan, which say they are Jews and are not, but do lie; behold, I will make them to come and worship before thy feet, and to know that I have loved thee.*
> **REVELATION 3:9 (KJV)**

These words, spoken by Jesus, expose false Jews and affirm the true identity of God's chosen people. This isn't symbolic—it's a direct warning and a call to spiritual awareness.

The deception didn't end in the first century. Today, many believe that the same spirit operates through the Amalekite, Khazarian, Luciferian, and Masonic groups—often called "the Illuminati." They are said to worship Lucifer, offering horrific sacrifices—including children—in exchange for power, wealth, and global influence. Their allegiance to evil is masked by prestige and prominence, but their works reveal their master.

Lucifer and his devotees twisted history, science, medicine, religion, and humanity itself to serve their will and destiny. Through blood communion with Lucifer, hellbent societies learned and used mind-destroying techniques to disempower humanity. These groups fostered a relationship with pure evil, and that evil taught them how to manipulate humanity, the money system, the religious system, and the medical system.

The members of the Illuminati are the real rulers of the world, and they have been pulling the strings from behind the scenes for centuries. They have infiltrated every government and every aspect of society around the planet. Some say that their ultimate goal is to install a satanic New World Order, a one-world government, that will prepare Earth's citizens for the coming of the antichrist. Their oath is as follows:

> I_____ take this oath that I_____ will follow the Illuminati rules and regulations and be honest to the New World Order of the Illuminati. I will help my fellow members in the fraternity and always respect and be faithful to those that are senior to me in the fraternity and that I _____ will always do whatever the high priests ask me to do, and try to do anything beyond or above the power of the Illuminati. I shall die and turn to a ram of the Oris, as I _____ take this oath, I _____have agreed to be a full member of the Illuminati, and my Lucifer bless me. So shall it be.

Satan and the fallen angels have always sought to corrupt human DNA and enslave mankind. This act is more than science—it's a direct assault on God's creation. Your DNA is the biological imprint of God, and altering it is a form of blasphemy against the Creator. The enemy's goal is confusion through unnatural mixing. Daniel 2:42 (KJV) declares, *"As the toes of the feet were partly of iron and partly of clay,"* symbolizing a forced union that was never meant to be. For decades, Satan has used media—TV, news, music, and the internet—to desensitize the world and prepare humanity to accept transhumanism: the merging of man and machine.

This agenda isn't random. In fact, it is the deliberate work of principalities and powers carried out through those who serve the god of this world. It's a closed club—and entry is by bloodline, not merit. These elites dictate what we believe, think, and consume. The table is tilted. The game is rigged. Yet most remain blind to it—and worse, many simply don't care. This ignorance and refusal to acknowledge what's happening only allows the evil to continue, and it's sometimes not even subtle. The Elites do tell us through their books, publications, movies, and news releases what they are doing; this is called "revelation of the method." If you are too stupid to recognize it for what it is, that is your problem from their point of view. It is a form of ritual mocking of the victim.

This mockery isn't accidental. It's part of a broader strategy to sow chaos, control perception, and keep the masses distracted while power is consolidated behind the scenes. Allegedly, billionaire George Soros spent $33M bankrolling Ferguson demonstrators to create echo chambers and drive national protests. He promises everyone who participates in the massive protest $15 an hour. All of this is to destabilize a country and to create division—by skin color, by political wing, by religion, and by gender. A divided people is easy to rule. We are making the job easier for them by looking the other way.

According to the U.S. Department of State, human trafficking is the fastest-growing criminal industry in the world, second to drug trafficking. This is modern-day slavery, which generates over $150B annually for organized crime. But behind the statistics lies a darker truth—one protected by power and concealed in plain sight. Allegedly, in 2010, Laura Gayler Silsby was found smuggling children out of Haiti. She was a member of the board of directors for "Alert Sense," the company that provides the technology for AMBER Alerts. She was caught stealing children in Haiti with the Clintons. She also founded a Baptist organization, New Life Refuge Ministers, a refuge mission for Haiti.

And the corruption didn't end there—it deepened. It

was said that $3M was diverted from Haiti in relief funds by the Clinton Foundation to pay for Chelsea's extravagant wedding. Allegedly, they pretended to assist Haiti after the earthquake but instead raped the country of billions of dollars. The Red Cross, owned by the Rothschilds, raised half a billion dollars for Haiti and only built six homes.

But those who get too close to the truth often pay the ultimate price. When Klaus Eberwein, a former governmental official of Haiti, was due to testify against the Clintons, he was found dead with a bullet in his head only days before the trial. Monica Petersen, an anthropologist who went to Haiti to investigate human trafficking on the island and tweeted some incriminating information about the Clinton Foundation, was also found dead by hanging. Her death was ruled a suicide.

And it didn't stop there. Allegedly, when surgeon Dean Lovich openly vented his disgust about the corruption happening within the Clinton Foundation—corruption he witnessed firsthand while trying to save lives—he, too, ended up dead.

NEW WORLD ORDER

Adam Weishaupt (1748 - 1811) formed the Order of Perfectibilists on May 1, 1776 (to this day celebrated as May Day throughout many western countries), which later became known as the Illuminati, a secret society whose name means "Enlightened Ones". Although the Order was founded to provide an opportunity for the free exchange of ideas, Weishaupt's background as a Jesuit seems to have influenced the actual character of the society, such that the express aim of this Order became to abolish Christianity, and overturn all civil government. While Weishaupt planted the seed, someone else turned it into a global agenda.

The creation of the New World Order (NWO) agenda was put in motion by the infamous figure Mayer Amschel Rothschild, the man who resolved to control the entire planet by any means necessary. His plan was not only ruthless; it was apocalyptic. Deception, control, financial enslavement, blackmail, and murder were merely the foundation. The deeper layers involved orchestrated wars, engineered famines, and a depopulation agenda pointing to a genocide unlike anything the world had seen.

The first step was unity through evil.

1773 – Rothschild assembled twelve of his most influential allies and persuaded them that they could dominate the world if they pooled their wealth and power. This secretive meeting took place in Frankfurt, Germany—and from it, a global web of influence began to take form. *But the plan wouldn't remain hidden forever.*

In 1933, the insignia of the Order of the Illuminati surfaced publicly—on the reverse side of the U.S. one-dollar bill. At the base of the 13-step pyramid appears the year 1776, marked in Roman numerals (MDCCLXXVI), signaling the official birth of the New World Order. Above the pyramid looms the all-seeing eye—Lucifer's eye—radiating control and surveillance in every direction. This is no mere symbol; it represents the rise of a terroristic, Gestapo-like agency of domination, first conceived by Adam Weishaupt and now embedded into the very currency of the Western world.

The Latin phrase "ANNUIT COEPTIS" means "our enterprise has been crowned with success," while "NOVUS ORDO SECLORUM" declares the goal: a New World Order. In 1933, 33rd-degree Freemason Franklin D. Roosevelt added the Great Seal to the U.S. dollar, turning it into an occult symbol. He also removed the nation from the gold standard and signed a gold confiscation order— consolidating control under the guise of economic reform. But the symbol predates America. It traces back to ancient secret societies and remains the emblem of the Freemasons to this day.

1821 – George W. F. Hegel formulated the Hegelian dialectic, which is the process by which Illuminati objectives are achieved. According to the Hegelian dialectic, thesis plus antithesis equals synthesis. In other words, first, the Elite creates a false crisis, regardless of the collateral damage.

Once there is an enormous public outcry, something must be done about the crisis or problem. They then claim to offer a solution that will ultimately bring about the changes they really wanted all along, but the people would think that it was because of their outcry and will willfully agree to the solution (which they would not have accepted initially), not realizing that it will be the country's downfall.

1828 – Mayer Amschel Rothschild, who financed the Illuminati, expressed his utter contempt for national governments that attempted to regulate International Bankers as he stated, "Allow me to issue and control the money of a nation, and I care not who writes the laws." But his war was not only against governments—it was against God Himself. Rothschild boldly declared, "We must war against all prevailing ideas of religion, of the state, of country, of patriotism. The idea of God is the keynote of a perverted civilization. It must be destroyed."

And so began a long-term, carefully calculated plan—one rooted in rebellion and carried out through control, deception, and manipulation. Their objectives are chillingly precise:

1. One World Government
2. One World Cashless Currency
3. One World Central Bank
4. One World Military
5. The elimination of national sovereignty
6. The abolition of all private property
7. The dismantling of the family unit
8. Depopulation through controlled population growth and density
9. Mandatory multiple vaccines
10. Universal basic income (austerity)

11. A microchipped society for purchasing, travel, and surveillance
12. Implementation of a global social credit system (like China)
13. Integration of all appliances into a 5G surveillance grid (Internet of Things)
14. Government-raised children
15. Government-controlled education from preschool through university
16. The end of private vehicle ownership
17. All businesses absorbed by state or corporate control
18. Restricted air travel deemed "nonessential"
19. Human settlement zones concentrated in dense urban areas
20. The end of irrigation and private agriculture
21. Elimination of private homes and independent land use
22. Bans on natural medicine and fossil fuels

This isn't a dystopian fantasy. It's a roadmap, a roadmap already in motion.

According to the claim, the United Nations' "Agenda 21/2030 Mission Goals" outline over 20 strategic objectives designed to advance the New World Order. The agenda includes one world government, a single cashless currency, government-owned and controlled schools, colleges, and universities, and an end to single-family homes. Sound familiar?

We have been immersed in an anti-democracy propaganda bubble for over a generation now. It's gotten to the point where people do not even understand that you cannot have a democracy when every interaction between citizens and increasingly fused government/corporations is reduced to domination by the powerful and compliance by the powerless.

Revelation 17 unveils a sobering truth: the Harlot—symbolic of the Roman Catholic Church—is a mystery to John because she presents herself as a Christian Church while working to deceive the world and destroy the saints. This deception is not isolated.

Revelation 13:1 (KJV) declares, *"And I saw a beast rise out of the sea, having seven heads and ten horns."* This beast represents Rome. The seven heads signify the seven mountains upon which the city sits, and the ten horns symbolize the European nations aligned with her. In prophecy, "beast" is a symbol for kingdoms. But the narrative intensifies.

Revelation 13:11–12 (KJV) says, *"And I beheld another beast (America) coming up out of the earth; and he had two horns like a lamb, and he spake as a dragon. And he exerciseth all the power of the first beast (Rome) before him, and causeth the earth and them which dwell therein to worship the first beast, whose deadly wound was healed."*

This reveals a terrifying alliance. The United States and Rome will unite church and state, enforcing laws that persecute the saints. Obedience to this system is not neutral; it is worship of the beast. They are called "Mystery, Babylon the Great" because their deception runs deep. They appear Christian on the surface, yet are rooted in the ancient Babylonian religion of sun worship and Satanic rituals.

Behind the mask of faith lies a darker agenda. The New World Order doesn't merely seek dominance. The New World Order seeks mass extermination, with plans to eliminate 90% of the global population.

TRUTH EXPOSED

We will identify those who have played an active role in either exposing Satan's agenda or being a direct participant in Satan's agenda.

TESTIMONY OF THE INSTITUTION OF MEDICINE

John D. Rockefeller, under the guise of humanitarianism, seized control of American media and reshaped the medical industry after discovering that pharmaceutical drugs could be manufactured from petroleum. As one of the nation's leading oil tycoons, he unleashed a propaganda machine to rewrite reality and push his profit-driven agenda.

Medicine used for thousands of years was suddenly classified as an alternative, while the new petroleum-based, highly addicted, and patentable drugs were declared the gold standard. Next, Rockefeller bought the German pharmaceutical company that manufactured chemicals of war for Adolf Hitler. He then leveraged his political influence by pressing Congress to declare natural healing maladies.

Rockefeller then took control of the American Medical Association and began offering massive grants to top medical schools under the mandate that only "his" approved curriculum was taught. Any mention of the healing powers of herbs, plants, and diets was erased from most medical textbooks. Doctors and professors who objected were crucified by the media, removed from the American Medical Association, stripped of their license, and/or arrested.

When evidence began to emerge that petroleum-based medicine was causing cancer, Rockefeller founded the American Cancer Society to suppress that information. He is duly credited as the founder of the pharmaceutical industry.

TESTIMONY OF HENRY FORD

As with most famous people, Henry Ford was complex and had traits and took actions that were laudatory as well as troublesome. The most controversial and least admirable aspect of Ford's career was his descent into anti-Semitism. Convinced that "bankers" and "the Jews" were responsible for a whole range of things he didn't like, from the world war to short skirts to jazz music, Ford used his newspaper, the Dearborn Independent, to carry on an active anti-Semitic campaign.

Between 1920 and 1922, a series of articles denounced all things Jewish. While officially apologizing for the articles in 1927, Ford's anti-Jewish sentiments ran deep. Seen within the context of the times, they demonstrated the sharp realities and tensions that emerge in societies undergoing profound cultural, economic, and political change.

Ford's paper, The Dearborn Independent, displayed on the front page every week, "The International Jew: The World's Problem," which examined a purported conspiracy launched by Jewish groups to achieve world domination. His crusade against World War I convinced him that international Jewish bankers were fomenting the war. Ford saw Jews present in everything that he viewed as modern and distasteful—contemporary music, movies, theater, new dress styles, and loosening social mores. Every week for nearly two years, the paper published articles that assailed Jews for being sneaky and treacherous and conspiring to control the global financial system.

Ford also implied that the Jews were scheming to dominate American industries such as Hollywood, farming, and liquor distribution. "There is no other racial or national type which puts forth this kind of person," the Dearborn Independent said in June 1920. "It is not merely that there are a few Jews among international financial controllers—it is that these world controllers are exclusively Jews."

TESTIMONY OF MICHAEL SWIFT

In 1987, Michael Swift was asked to contribute an editorial piece to Gay Community News (GCN), an important gay community magazine, although well to the left of most American gay and lesbian opinion. A decade later, this text, printed in the Congressional Record, is repeatedly cited, apparently verbatim, by the religious right as evidence of the "Gay Agenda." The "Gay Revolutionary" states:

> *We shall sodomize your sons, emblems of your feeble masculinity, of your shallow dreams and vulgar lies. We shall seduce them in your schools, in your dormitories, in your gymnasiums, in your locker rooms, in your army bunkhouses, in your truck stops, in your male clubs, in your houses of Congress, wherever men are with men together. Your sons shall become our minions and do our bidding. They will be recast in our image. They will come to crave and adore us.*
>
> *All laws banning homosexual activity will be revoked. We will unmask the powerful homosexuals who masquerade as heterosexuals. We shall raise vast private armies, as Mishima*

did, to defeat you. We shall conquer the world because warriors inspired by and banded together by homosexual love and honor are invincible as were the ancient Greek soldiers.

While it may have been intended as satire, this is not satire; it is a manifesto. It exposes a radical desire not for equality but for domination—rooted in the deconstruction of traditional values, the reshaping of young minds, and the deliberate erasure of moral and spiritual foundations.

TESTIMONY OF ALBERT PIKE

An Italian revolutionary leader, Giuseppe Mazzini (1805-1872), a 33rd degree Mason, was selected by the Illuminati to head their worldwide operations in 1834. (Mazzini also founded the Mafia in 1860). Because of Mazzini's revolutionary activities in Europe, the Bavarian government cracked down on the Illuminati and other secret societies for allegedly plotting a massive overthrow of Europe's monarchies. As the secrets of the Illuminati were revealed, they were persecuted and eventually disbanded, only to re-establish themselves in the depths of other organizations, of which Freemasonry was one.

Mazzini enticed Albert Pike into the (now formally disbanded but still operating) Illuminati. Pike was fascinated by the idea of a one-world government, and when asked by Mazzini, readily agreed to write a ritual tome that guided the transition from average high-ranking mason into a top-ranking Illuminati mason (33rd degree). Since Mazzini also wanted Pike to head the Illuminati's American chapter, he clearly felt Pike was worthy of such a task.

Pike was said to be a Satanist who indulged in the occult, and he apparently possessed a bracelet which he used to summon Lucifer, with whom he had constant communication. He was the Grand Master of a Luciferian group known as the Order of the Palladium (or Sovereign Council of Wisdom), which had been founded in Paris in 1737.

Albert Pike received a vision, which he described in a letter that he wrote to Mazzini, dated August 15, 1871. This letter graphically outlined plans for three world wars that were seen as necessary to bring about the One World Order, and we can marvel at how accurately it has predicted events that have already taken place.

What follows is a chilling breakdown of these predicted global conflicts, each strategically designed to reshape the world and pave the way for total domination.

The First World War must be brought about to permit the Illuminati to overthrow the power of the Czars in Russia and to make that country a fortress of atheistic Communism. The divergences caused by the "Agentur" (agents) of the Illuminati between the British and Germanic Empires will be used to foment this war. At the end of the war, Communism will be built and used to destroy the other governments and to weaken the religions.

The Second World War must be fomented by taking advantage of the differences between the Fascists and the political Zionists. This war must be brought about so that Nazism is destroyed and the political Zionism be strong enough to institute a sovereign state of Israel in Palestine. During the Second World War, International Communism must become strong enough to balance Christendom, which would then be restrained and held in check until the time when we would need it for the final social cataclysm.

The Third World War must be fomented by taking advantage of the differences caused by the "Agentur" of the "Illuminati" between the political Zionists and the leaders of the Islamic World. The war must be conducted in such a way that Islam and political Zionism mutually destroy each other. Meanwhile, the other nations, once more divided on this issue, will be constrained to fight to the point of complete physical, moral, spiritual, and economic exhaustion.

We shall unleash the Nihilists and the atheists, and we shall provoke a formidable social cataclysm which, in all its horror, will show clearly to the nations the effect of absolute atheism, the origin of savagery, and the bloodiest turmoil.

This manifestation will result from the general reactionary movement, which will follow the destruction of Christianity and atheism, both conquered and exterminated at the same time.

TESTIMONY OF ALICE BAILEY

While the church sleeps, the devil is damaging souls with the Babylonian system. Here is a strategy crafted by an occultist, Alice Ann Bailey (June 16, 1880 – December 15, 1949). Alice Bailey was the leader of the Luciferian Society who created the 10-point charter set to destroy the traditional Judeo Christianity and lay the foundation of the New Age Movement. With calculated intent, she outlined a strategic blueprint to dismantle biblical values from the inside out:

1. **Take God And Prayer Out Of The Education System**

    Change curriculum to ensure that children are freed from the bondage of Christian culture. If you take God out of education, they will unconsciously form a resolve that God is not necessary to face life. Today, they introduce Transcendental Meditation (TM) in schools, which takes children to altered states of consciousness to meet with demons or spirit guides, equaling a New Age.

2. **Reduce Parental Authority Over The Children**

    Break the communication between parent and child.

Why? So that parents do not pass on their Christian traditions to their children and liberate children from the bondage of their parent traditions.

- *Promote excessive child rights.* (Between 1997 and 1998, South Africa introduced child rights legislation, which is supported through the UNICEF Charter. Today, a child can tell a parent, "I do not want to hear that; I don't want to do what you're telling me." Teachers are unable to discipline students, as children now assert, "I have my rights—you cannot talk to me like that.")
- *Abolish corporal punishment.* This abolishment has been made law. Modern policies promoting excessive child rights oppose biblical instruction. The Bible clearly states, "Do not withhold correction from a child, for if you beat him with a rod, he will not die. You shall beat him with a rod, and deliver his soul from hell" (Proverbs 23:13–14 NKJV).
- *Teachers are the agents of implementation.* From workshops, teachers tell children, "Your parent has no right to force you to pray or read the Bible; you are yourself, have a right of your own, you need to discover yourself, self-expression, self-realization, self-fulfillment are all buzz words." In the West, when the child is seven years old, the teachers begin to say to the child, "You have a right to choose whether you want to follow the faith of your parents or not; parents are not allowed to enforce their faith upon you." The question is, what type of decision can a 7-year-old make?

3. **Destroy The Judeo-Christian Family Structure Or The Traditional Christian Family Structure**

   It is oppressive, and the family is the core of the nation. If you break the family, you break the nation. Liberate the people from the confines of this structure. How?

   - *Promote sexual promiscuity.* The promotion encourages young people to embrace premarital sex, celebrates "free sex," and elevates it as life's greatest pleasure. Society is taught to fantasize about sex, glorify it, and take pride in being sexually active—even outside of marriage.
   - *Use the advertising industry, media – TV, magazines, and film industry to promote sexual enjoyment as the highest pleasure in humanity.* Even when they advertise ice cream, they must show you a woman's thigh and a bikini; they must do something to set off a trail of thoughts. They will show you more thighs than ice cream.

4. **If Sex Is Free, Then Make Abortion Legal And Make It Easy**

   Build clinics for abortion—health clinics in schools. If people are going to enjoy the joy of sexual relationships, they need to be free of unnecessary fears; in other words, they should not be hampered with unwanted pregnancies. Today, it is not only accessible but also forced. Today, abortion is a strategy to curb population control, together with the use of condoms and pills.

5. **Make Divorce Easy And Legal, Free People From The Concept Of Marriage For Life.**

   To completely uproot the sanctity of marriage, it must be treated as disposable. By making divorce effortless and socially acceptable, covenant is replaced with convenience, and long-term commitment becomes a thing of the past.

6. **Make Homosexuality An Alternative Lifestyle**

Over 65 years ago, Alice Bailey promoted the idea that sexual pleasure is the highest form of human fulfillment. She argued that no one should be denied or restricted in how they choose to experience it. People should be free to engage in any form of sexual expression, including homosexuality, incest, or even bestiality, as long as there is mutual consent.

7. **Debase Art, Make It Run Mad**

How? Promote new forms of art that will corrupt and defile the imagination of people because art is the language of the spirit, that which is inside; you can bring out in painting, music, drama, etc. Look at the quality of the music that is coming out, the films out of Hollywood.

8. **Use Media To Promote And Change Mindset**

The media is the most influential source you need to use to change human attitudes. Use the press, the radio, TV, and cinema. So much money is pumped into media and advertising, spreading pornographic material and other sources.

9. **Create An Interfaith Movement**

Promote all religions as equal to Christianity and dismantle the belief that Jesus is the only way to salvation. In doing so, the exclusive truth of the Gospel is diluted, Christianity is gradually discredited, and other faiths are elevated in its place—leading many away from the narrow path that leads to eternal life.

10. Get Governments To Make All These Laws And Get The Church To Endorse These Changes.

The church must change its doctrine and accommodate the people by accepting these things and putting them into its structures and systems.

Today, you wonder why our governments are legislating laws contrary to the Bible and why the church is compromising the Word of God. It is a process of implementing The Plan - A 50-year strategy of the New Age Movement to fulfill its ultimate goal to establish a One World Government, a One World Economic system, and a One World Religion.

Today, the strategy has almost been entirely adopted by the United Nations, and much of it is already the law in many nations. This deception has crept up unobserved on so many people. It can best be demonstrated through the well-known analogy of the frog in the pot of water. If you put a frog in a pot of boiling water, it is smart enough to know that it is in terrible danger and will immediately jump out to safety. But if you turn up the heat very slowly, a little at a time, it doesn't notice the changes taking place and will slowly cook to death. Many people today are slowly cooking to death and don't seem to realize how far they have come from where they once were.

Interestingly, Blavatsky, Besant, and Alice Bailey (1880 -1949) were well-known Masonic leaders of the day. Albert Pike referred to Freemasonry as the 'custodian' or special guardian of these occult secrets and revealed the hidden agenda of his institution, the forming of a Luciferic One World Government.

TESTIMONY OF THE KING ALFRED PLAN

You are about to read information extracted from the U.S. Library of Congress by researchers in Ohio, Pennsylvania, and California. Due to the sinister objectives outlined in the data, disclosure to the Black and Hispanic communities is obligatory. The National Security Council developed a new government program between 1960 and 1964. It is called "The King Alfred Plan."

The plan details the encampment and extermination of 22 million Blacks (U.S. census count for 1970). President Reagan had solidified it under Louis Giuffrida, ex-director of the Federal Emergency Management Agency (FEMA). The plan is under the control of FEMA and had been secured under executive orders 11490, 11921, and 12148 and amended under National Security Directive #52 (aka REX-84) as of April 6, 1984.

At the point when government abuse triggers riots and revolution among Black communities and other people of color around the world, a presidential order will activate what's known as the King Alfred Plan—or, as it will be officially called, "The National Crisis" or "National Emergency." At that moment, multiple agencies—including the National Security Council, Central Intelligence Agency, Federal Bureau of Investigation, Department of Justice, Department of Defense, Department of the Interior, National Guard units, and state, county, and city police departments—will be mobilized to execute the plan.

In addition, in 1982, Oliver North and President Reagan added an amendment to the King Alfred plan entitled "REX-84" (signed into law in 1984) which provides that Latinos be included in the extermination and that the Neo-Nazi groups in Texas, Louisiana, and Mississippi be federally funded and trained so that when the President declares The National Crisis, these groups will be immediately deputized to assist law enforcement in the round-up and incarceration.

I already know your reactions: the sophisticated will laugh at the outrageousness of it all; the pacifists will continue as if they never knew; the thinkers will become angry and try to intellectualize a way out; the fighters will say, "I ain't goin' out like that!" and arm themselves to the teeth. But how are you going to fight? We have no military, no munitions plants, no Black banking system, no food production system, and definitely no land base! They have already planned to use gas, radiation, chemically altered food and water, and ultra-low sound waves to incapacitate you.

There is only one way out: Ecclesiastes 12:13 (KJV) says, "Let us hear the conclusion of the whole matter: Fear God and keep his commandments: for this is the whole duty of man."

CONCLUSION

We have been immersed in an anti-democracy propaganda bubble for several generations now. It's gotten to the point where people do not even understand that you cannot have a democracy when every interaction between citizens and increasingly fused government and corporations is reduced to domination by the powerful and compliance by the powerless.

There has been a noticeable rise in immorality, a blatant disregard for ethical standards, and an erosion of the values that once held society together; the increase in violent corruption and depravity is not just reported in the news, but it is visible in most urban communities, schools, and workplaces. The fabric of society is fraying, and this moral decline is an indicator that we are living in unprecedented times. The illusion of freedom will continue if it's profitable to continue the illusion. At the point where the illusion becomes too expensive to maintain, they will just take down the scenery, they will pull back the curtains, they will move the tables and chairs out of the way, and you will see the brick wall at the back of the theater. Lies are exalted, and truth is hunted down. Let's stop worshipping the creature (Satan) and worship the Creator (The Most High God).

There are only two kingdoms:

One is the Kingdom of Darkness. It says in John 10:10 that Satan's kingdom leads us to deception, death, and destruction. The Bible also refers to the "domain of darkness" as the realm of demons, including Satan, who control the Earth's belief systems and try to deceive and destroy people.

The other is the Kingdom of God (Light), where you reign in life by grace, through righteousness, in which Christ rules. You are in one or the other. There are no in-betweens. You are in the fight whether you want to be or not—so choose your kingdom. You will die if you remain on the Titanic listening to the music!

Deuteronomy 30:19 (KJV) says, *"I call heaven and earth to record this day against you, that I have set before you life and death, blessing and cursing: therefore choose life, that both thou and thy seed may live: That thou mayest love the Lord thy God, and that thou mayest obey his voice, and that thou mayest cleave unto him: for he is thy life, and the length of thy days: that thou mayest dwell in the land which the Lord sware unto thy fathers, to Abraham, to Isaac, and to Jacob, to give them."*

Enoch 98:7–8 (KJV) warns, *"Do not deceive yourselves by thinking in your heart that your sins go unnoticed—that you do not see or know. Every sin is recorded daily in Heaven before the Most High. From now on, understand that all your wrongdoing is written down each day, until the day of judgment."*

How is it that many of us readily obey man's corrupt laws—designed to hinder, oppress, and destroy—yet refuse to obey God's righteous laws, which are meant to bless, elevate, and give us life?

Deuteronomy 28:1 (KJV) informs us, *"If thou will obey the commandments of the LORD thy God, I will set thee on high above all nations of the earth."*

Why, in America, can you deny Christ as the Messiah and the existence of the Most High God without any repercussion, but you cannot deny the Holocaust or be Anti-Zionist without being criminalized as antisemitic?

Hosea 4:6 (KJV) says, *"My people are destroyed for lack of knowledge: because thou hast rejected knowledge, I will also reject thee."*

Open your eyes and look around—who has been targeted and systematically destroyed since being kidnapped and brought to America? Answer: Black Americans.

Think it not strange what you see unfolding around you—these are the last days.

America offers you nothing but death. He who has an ear to hear, let him hear.

I close with Galatians 4:16 (KJV): *"Am I therefore become your enemy, because I tell you the truth?"*

So be it. If truth makes me your enemy, then let the truth stand. But know this—what you reject today may be the very truth that could have saved you. The time for comfort has passed. Judgment is near. Choose wisely… while you still can.

THE AUTHOR'S THOUGHTS

W e have been turned upside down and inside out. We don't know who we are, we don't know our true culture, our true religion, who God is, or what dispensation of time we are living in. We would rather trust in this Babylonian, Beast system called America. We would rather believe and trust the men and women who govern the world. This governmental system programmed and brainwashed our minds and then told us what to believe, what to think. They indoctrinated us as opposed to educating us according to their ideology and not according to the Bible. The government set up many of our Black churches. Our pastors learned from their institutions, including their seminary schools, and they were instructed on what to preach. This is why Christianity has grossly failed, because most of our preachers have always been the tools of the government against the people. We need to look at the world through God's eyes and not man's lies.

For centuries, men accepted the idea that all things were created by God, an all-wise, all-powerful being, and that He is in control of the earth and all things upon it. But as education became more widespread, men began to question the theories accepted by their forefathers and to turn to their own reasoning. It is difficult for a finite man with his limited understanding to visualize an infinite God—eternal, unchanging, unsearchable, all-powerful, all-knowing, invisible to human eyes. The very existence of life is evidence of God's existence. Of his own power, man is incapable of creating even the smallest living thing. He cannot create himself. A being greater than himself created him. No life exists without a creator. Life must have come from a higher power. Only God can give life. The God of the Bible is a real being. He is a living, active, forceful, radiant personality whom the angels—who are also real beings—bow in reverence and praise. To Him belongs ALL authority and power. He has NO equal; He is the One, the Supreme, the Divine Being.

Have you ever wondered? Why is it that everyone, all nations of people, are always concerned about Black Americans? We are the topic of discussion among every ethnic group. We are the center of attention for all nations. The whole world watches us, and the entire world copies us. What is it about Black Americans? You will find that answer in my first book, "I Can't Breathe, Don't Die Twice." America never wanted us to leave. There was always a fear of our joining in an alliance with another nation and/or retaliation against them. If we left, then who would fuel their economy and their capitalistic system? We have been since slavery, and still today, their money-making machine and all facets of life.

Wake up, Americans, particularly so-called Black Americans—you are in a spiritual, physical, and psychological war. Ephesians 6:11-13 (NIV) says, "Put on the full armor of God, so that you can take your stand against the devil's schemes. For our struggle is not against flesh and blood, but against the rulers, against the authorities, against the powers of this dark world and against the spiritual forces of evil in the heavenly realms. Therefore, put on the full armor of God, so that when the day of evil comes (which is already in operation in the earth) you may be able to stand your ground." The unknown war—dis-ease: movies (subliminal messages), COVID, chem-trails, censorship, depopulation, weather control, and global warming.

Black Americans, your fight is not about using weapons of men, but weapons of the Most High God. The Bible tells us to put on the whole armor of God. But you must first understand who you are and understand the tactics and warfare of your enemy. I outlined in this book the ultimate enemy: Satan, the fallen angels, demons, and their cohorts. Psalms 83 details for us our enemies and their plans against us.

We were placed under a demonic spell, but it's time to wake up and be aware. We must repent and come out of sin, acknowledge Christ as our King and Savior, who is soon to return. Satan will continue to rule and win if we continue to remain in sin. This is urgent, for the world is soon coming to an end.

CONNECT WITH THE AUTHOR

Thank you for reading, *Still Can't Breathe: Unbelievable Deception.* Be sure to check out the first book of this series: *I Can't Breathe, Don't Die Twice,* available on Amazon and other online book retailers. To connect with the author, email: deb8laster@yahoo.com.